LET'S VISIT ICELAND

Let's visit
ICELAND

I.O.EVANS

BURKE

First published October 1976
Revised new edition 1983
© I.O. Evans 1976
New material in this edition © Burke Publishing Company Limited 1983

ACKNOWLEDGEMENTS

The author and publishers are grateful to the Iceland Tourist Information Bureau for permission to reproduce the illustrations in this book.

CIP data
Evans, I.O.
    Let's visit Iceland. – 2nd ed.
    1.   Iceland – Social life and customs – Juvenile literature
    I.   Title
    949.1'204   DL326
    ISBN 0 222 00926 8

Burke Publishing Company Limited
Pegasus House, 116–120 Golden Lane, London EC1Y 0TL, England.
Burke Publishing (Canada) Limited
Toronto, Ontario, Canada.
Burke Publishing Company Inc.
540 Barnum Avenue, Bridgeport, Connecticut 06608, U.S.A.
Filmset in 'Monophoto' Baskerville by Green Gates Studios, Hull, England.
Printed in Singapore by Tien Wah Press (Pte) Ltd.

Contents

ICELAND

ARCT

Snaefells

Hvalfjördur

REYKJAVIK

Keflavik

Krisuvik

Bessastadir

Geys

WESTMANN IS

Surtsey

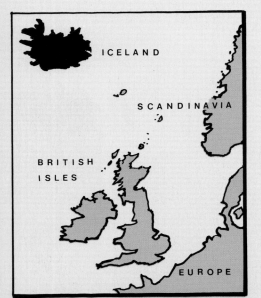

ICELAND

SCANDINAVIA

BRITISH
ISLES

EUROPE

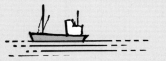

ATLANTIC OCE

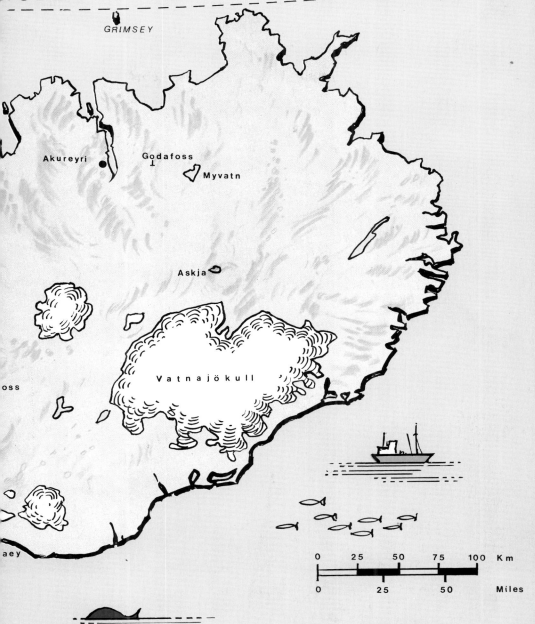

RCLE

GRIMSEY

Akureyri

Godafoss

Myvatn

Askja

Vatnajökull

oss

aey

0   25   50   75   100 Km

0   25   50   Miles

One of Iceland's most spectacular glaciers

Land of Frost and Fire

Iceland is situated in the North Atlantic, just south of the Arctic Circle. It is a large island, shaped something like a duck —the head is formed by a great peninsula on the north-west separated from the rest of the island by two large bays. Iceland's total area is 103,000 square kilometres (over 39,700 square miles), one fifth greater than that of Ireland. It is 278 kilometres (under 250 miles) from Greenland and 970 kilometres (nearly 600 miles) from Norway. Its capital, Reykjavik (*j* in Icelandic is always pronounced as the *y* in *yellow*) is roughly midway between Moscow and New York "as the crow (and the aeroplane) flies".

Only about one-quarter of the area of Iceland is habitable; the rest consists of barren mountains, raised deserts, lava-flows, and glaciers—some of which are covered with perpetual snow. These arid areas are mostly in the centre. The long coastline is broken by deep fjords which penetrate far inland, especially in the north-west peninsula. In the south and south-west there are lowlands, and it is here that most of the inhabitants live. These regions consist of silt deposited by the sea, whereas the rest of Iceland was formed by the cooling down of molten material from within the earth.

The cooled lava-flows are like the surface of the sea converted into solid rock; they resemble the surface of the moon, and the American astronauts got part of their training here. Instead of the rolling billows of the ocean, there are low ridges of rock;

9

instead of breaking waves, there are ridges resembling waves about to break—some of them so large that they would form good shelter for anyone who was marooned on the lava-flows; instead of the sea-spray, clouds of volcanic ash blow over the country, causing a nuisance on the gravel roads. An approaching car may be seen from some distance away because of the cloud of ash it raises, and vehicles have sometimes had all their paintwork stripped off because of friction from the clouds of ash.

Iceland was largely formed by volcanic eruptions, and some of the volcanoes are still active. In 1961 an eruption occurred at Askja, not far from the town of Akureyri in northern Iceland. In a few days it had died away and Askja became, as before, a snow-covered hill. Other eruptions have occurred at Hekla in the south (in 1947 and 1970) and off Heimaey, the principal island of the Westmann Islands, just south of Iceland (in 1963); this latter resulted in the formation of a new islet.

On January 23rd, 1973, a destructive eruption devastated much of Heimaey: a great fissure, 1·5 kilometres (about one mile) long, opened on the outskirts of the town, Iceland's most important fishing centre. Nearly eight thousand people had to be evacuated. The eruption continued until June 28th, and by then about one-third of the town and about four hundred houses had been buried or burnt by lava and volcanic bombs. The town has now been rebuilt. Yet another eruption occurred in early 1976 near Myvatn.

The country is still troubled with earthquakes, which sometimes accompany the volcanic outbursts. It is traversed by the

Hekla erupting. Note the lava belching out at the foot
of the eruption column, to the left

mid-Atlantic ridge—a wide crack in the earth's crust, mostly below sea-level. The geologists say that there is some danger that strains within the earth may become so great that they will split the whole island in half. Many of the Icelanders know this but it does not worry them at all. People who have been accustomed to thoughts of volcanoes and earthquakes ever since their land was first inhabited are not likely to be troubled by the distant prospect of such a catastrophe!

Volcanoes and earthquakes are formed by the earth's internal heat, which escapes here where the earth's crust is thin and weak. Fortunately, this thinness of the crust has more attractive results too. Among these are the geysers (spurts of hot water and steam shooting out of the ground) and hot springs. The latter range from boiling to pleasantly warm water, mingled with such things as sulphur and hot mud.

The most famous of these is the Great Geysir (geyser), at some distance to the east of Reykjavik. (Its name comes from the Icelandic word *geysa* meaning "to burst out violently". The general term "geysir" comes from this. The Great Geysir used to spout quite regularly, but now its activity is less predictable. However, there are other smaller geysers in Iceland.

Hveragerthi, also east of Reykjavik, is a small village in whose main street there is a geyser which has been "tamed"— it has been fitted with an internal pipe and with a thick metal cover which holds back the boiling water. When tourists arrive from Reykjavik and want to see the geyser in action, the cover is removed and a packet of soap is thrown in. It

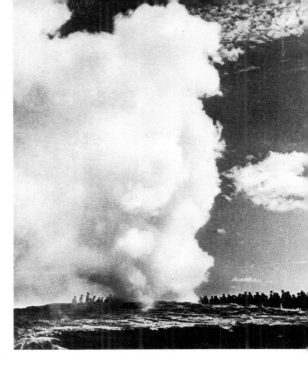

The Great Geysir

immediately emits a spurt about ten times the height of a man, to the great astonishment of the tourists. Then it is covered up again.

The water from the geyser is used to supply the houses and a greenhouse, in which grapes, tomatoes and exotic flowers are grown—plants from more temperate lands flourishing not far from the Arctic Circle!

The hot water from the geysers is also used for more important purposes—to warm whole towns, including Reykjavik itself. The water is filtered to remove impurities, stored in great reservoirs, and piped across country to local waterworks. From there is it distributed to homes, factories, and offices, and to warm swimming-baths. It smells and tastes faintly of sulphur, but it is not at all unpleasant, and Iceland's cold water —drawn from springs and streams—is quite fresh.

There are two distinct types of water in some of the streams and lakes: the water which comes from the geysers and hot springs is tinted slightly with blue from tiny particles of rock; that which comes from the melt-water of the glaciers is colourless and transparent. In some of the streams there are currents of two different colours flowing side by side.

Iceland's rocks do not contain coal, oil or natural gas. True, they contain many important ores, but the country's great mineral wealth consists of its supplies of water, welling from the ground or derived from the melting snow and ice, and of its underground heat. Its rivers and waterfalls and the jets of high-pressure steam could be used to generate electricity. Then shiploads of such minerals as alumina and bauxite could be imported from abroad to be smelted.

A great hydro-electric generating station is being constructed on a tributary of the Thjorsa River, near Hekla It should produce enough electricity for the whole of south-west Iceland and for a large aluminium smelting plant.

Though at one time the country was well-wooded, because of changes in the climate, too much tree-felling, and the destruction of the young shoots by sheep, it now has very few trees. There are, however, two plantations, mostly of birch, with some willow.

In spite of its name, Iceland is not a cold country. It is kept pleasantly temperate by the warm waters of the Gulf Stream.

There are a few spells of frost in winter and spring. Snow falls chiefly on the mountains. It is, however, windy with some gales and there can be rain-spells. Because of its high latitude, summer days are long and nights short. The spring and autumn are very long. In winter the days are short and the nights long. It is especially dark from mid-November to the end of January.

The air of Iceland is very clear, there is no industrial smoke or "smog", and in the northern latitudes the light is very good, so that in summer it seems almost brilliant. If you visit the country you may well wish to wear dark glasses; and if you take photographs you should "stop down" your lens or use shorter exposures to avoid over-exposing your snaps.

The midnight sun, near Reykjavik. At this high latitude the summer days are almost endless and the nights are very short

History

Iceland was almost unknown in Continental Europe until, during the fourth century B.C. a Greek scientist, Pytheas, sailed from Marseilles through the "Pillars of Hercules"—the Straits of Gibraltar—into the Bay of Biscay. Dodging the Carthaginian pirates, he turned northwards up the coasts of Spain and France, to the Tin Islands, which we now call the British Isles—(he mentions their "extremely chilly climate").

While there, he heard of, and may even have visited, *Ultima Thule*—"the farthest known region". Here, he said, there were no proper crops, and no cattle; the people lived on wild berries and millet, and their drink was mead prepared from honey. The nights were only two or three hours long. Beyond this was a "curdled sea", where nobody could either walk or swim; he compared it to a "sea-lung", for it heaved as though some monster were breathing below the surface.

Naturally, this did not sound very likely to his contemporaries, but the modern explorer Nansen said it was a very good description of the ice-sludge formed along the edge of the drift-ice, ground to a pulp by the waves and seen dimly through the damp grey Arctic mists.

It is not clear which country Pytheas was referring to. It *may* have been Norway, but it might easily have been Iceland.

The earliest people known to have visited Iceland were some Irish monks who arrived there during the eighth century. They may have followed, in their boats, the annual migration of the geese to their summer breeding-grounds. Aided by a favourable wind, and following the "skeins" of birds, they may have found their way there easily.

They were seeking for "the Island of Saints", but they too reached a sea which seemed to be clogged, and they saw a column, so high that it seemed to pierce the sky, made of the clearest crystal and as hard as rock—a large iceberg. Then, on the shore, they saw something even more terrible: a demon blacksmith seemed to tower up by the shore and to pelt them with burning rocks. There was a smell of sulphur, and a din as though the blacksmith were stoking up his forge—this was probably Mount Hekla in eruption. But their leader, St Brendan, raised his cross and, fortified by their prayers, the monks got away safely.

At Bessastadir, south of Reykjavik, is a modern church built on the site of an older one. Among its stained glass windows is one showing St Brendan holding up his cross and confronting the "demon blacksmith".

The monks were alarmed at the next new arrivals, and so cruised on further west to Greenland. The newcomers were the heathen Vikings from Norway. Being great lovers of freedom and used to self-government, they felt that the rule of King Harold Fairhair was oppressive, and they sought freedom across the sea. They landed in the north of Scotland and Ireland and, in spite of their love of freedom, when they landed they captured wives and slaves from the local people. This is why the population of Iceland is rather mixed.

In about A.D. 880 a "great Viking", Naddodd, was driven westward to a land which seemed to be uninhabited; it looked so wintry that he called it Snowland. Later Garda, a Swede, also driven off-course by storms, cruised round this country and proved that it was an island; he found it so pleasant that later he returned and made his home there.

Another "great Viking", Floki, went via the Shetlands to look for "Garda's Holme" (Garda's island). He had taken three ravens with him and he released them one by one. The third, instead of returning to the ship, flew onwards, showing that there was land ahead. Floki coasted round it, and when from a mountain summit he saw a glacier, he called the country Iceland. He found a few monks and priests there, with some Irish emigrants, and called them "Papar".

The Vikings were used to snow and ice and barren areas. There were not used to spurts of boiling water and jets of lava emerging from the earth, but such things did not daunt them.

A stone and turf hut such as the Vikings built

In the south, beside the many fjords, and along the coast, they found fertile soil. Off the shores and in the rivers there were plenty of fish. Here, above all, they were free from Harold Fairhair; so here many of them made their homes.

Prominent among them was the chieftain Ingolfur Arnanson: the first Viking to make his home in Iceland. When he arrived he threw the high pillars of his seat overboard, declaring that he would settle wherever they drifted ashore. In about 874 he found them off a region which seemed full of smoke (it was really the steam rising from the hot springs) so he called the settlement he founded Reykjavik—"Smoky Bay". In the eighteenth century this settlement became the capital of Iceland.

At first, each village and each group of farms in Iceland made its own laws, based on those of Norway, and its leading men formed a council called a "Thing". From 930 onwards, the leading men of all Iceland began to hold regular meetings of the "Al-Thing" at an inland valley named Thingvellir. This is the oldest Parliament in the world—the British Parliament at Westminster is sometimes called "The Mother of Parliaments", but the Icelandic Al-Thing could be called "The Grandmother of Parliaments", for it is older still!

Here laws were made for the whole country—in A.D. 1000, for example, it was decided here that Iceland should become a Christian country; it was however agreed that those who wished to go on worshipping the old heathen gods might continue to do so—provided they did so only in private.

The Al-Thing was not only a solemn assembly for law-making and for trying law-breakers and ordering their punishment, it was also a rallying-point for business, recreation and sport. Here fairs were held and goods bought and sold; here athletic displays and competitions were organised; here marriages were arranged. It was more than a Parliament: it was for the Icelanders what the original Olympic Games were for the Greeks and what the Eisteddfod is to the modern Welsh.

Unfortunately, even the Al-Thing did not enable the country's leaders to agree, and the King of Norway took advantage of the quarrels to bring them under his power. In 1262 the Icelanders even swore an oath of allegiance to him. Then the Norwegians began to interfere with the country's trade. Meantime, perhaps because the climate was getting colder, agriculture suffered, and life in Iceland, never very easy, began to get really hard.

It got even worse when, in 1380, Iceland as well as Norway, came under the rule of the King of Denmark. The Norwegians had, after all, regarded the Icelanders as their kinsmen; but the Danes had no feelings of kinship for them, so they treated them as a subject people. They meddled in Icelandic affairs, forcing the country to accept the Reformation and interfering with its trade. They treated it much as the British later treated their American colonies, but the Americans could and did rebel; the Icelanders were powerless to do so. They had no army and no navy; their only weapons were knives, harpoons and a few shot-guns, and their only vessels were fishing-smacks. They were also unable to protect themselves against pirates from Spain, Algeria and England. Never wealthy, they now became poverty-stricken.

Worst of all was the great fissure eruption of 1783, when the earth opened not in an ordinary crater but in a vast chasm thirty-two kilometres (nearly twenty miles) long. Great floods of molten lava gushed out. These, with showers of volcanic ash and the clouds of noxious gas, killed many Icelanders and threatened to destroy the others by killing their cattle and ruining their crops. This was the most extensive lava-flow ever recorded. So great was the devastation that even the harsh Danish government was moved to pity and seriously thought of evacuating the survivors and re-settling them in Denmark.

After 1800 the Al-Thing ceased to meet, and it must have seemed as if Iceland were in danger of losing its freedom. But the stalwart Icelanders were unwilling to leave their island home. Devastated though it was by the fissure eruption, Iceland was *their* country and they were not going to forsake it. Even when most oppressed by the Danes they had never lost the Viking love of freedom. During the nineteenth century, they began, like many of the oppressed people of Europe, to demand the right to govern themselves.

They were headed by Jon Sigurdsson, a great scholar and statesman, who stood up for them against their Danish rulers. Thanks to his efforts they won their freedom peacefully. Though still under the rule of Denmark, their trade was freed in 1853, they were granted a constitution, and in 1874 their

This modest grey building in Reykjavik is now the home of the Icelandic Parliament. (To the right of the picture is the cathedral).

Al-Thing was revived (it was however moved from Thing-vellir to a Parliament Building in Reykjavik). Standards of living improved and the population increased.

After the end of the First World War in 1918, an Act of Union was signed between Denmark and Iceland. Under this, both countries were declared independent, though they would still be united under the Danish King, and for the time being fishery protection and foreign affairs would still be handled by Denmark. The Icelanders decided that their country should have no army, only a police force, and no navy except for a few small lightly-armed gunboats to protect the fishing fleet. They also decided that Iceland would be neutral in any war.

This, however, was easier said than dne
land which is in a strategic position to dominate
and airways of the North Atlantic! In May 1940 the
were not pleased to find their streets swarming with B
soldiers, who had arrived to protect them from occupation
by the Germans. About a year later, the British troops were
replaced by men from the United States, who still occupy a
small NATO (North Atlantic Treaty Organisation) base at
Keflavik, near the tip of the peninsula which extends west of
Reykjavik.

In 1944, at the end of the Second World War, the Icelanders
decided, by an overwhelming vote, that they would break
their association with Denmark. Iceland now became an
independent self-governing Republic, a member of the
United Nations and of NATO, co-operating with Scandinavia
through the Nordic Council.

No longer do the Icelanders hope to keep always neutral.
They have to face not only their own special problems but
those of the rest of the world. They are facing them with the
same determination which their ancestors showed when
they refused to leave their land even after it had been devastated by the fissure eruption nearly two hundred years ago,
and which their Viking forefathers had displayed when, over a
thousand years ago, they had set out to make their home in
this strange island where the volcanoes flared among the
snowfields beneath the lurid glare of the Northern Lights.

eland and know little about it
as Eskimoes, but there are no
ive in Greenland or in North
)es are not really white, whereas
ne white race known as the Cau-
egian stock, being the descendants of
the   e Icelanders are of pure Norwegian
blood, how   eir ancestors captured and took with
them to Iceland a imber of Celts. So some Icelanders are
distantly related to the modern Scots and Irish.

Most Icelanders are tall, fair and blue-eyed, though some, partly of Celtic descent, are shorter and darker. Like the Vikings, they are great lovers of sport and of the open air and the sea—and they also have Viking appetitites!

Their language is difficult to learn, for it has changed little since the Vikings first settled in Iceland. Apart from a few modern words it is still used in much the same form as when the Icelandic sagas—age-old epic poems—were composed. Nevertheless, modern terms are translated into Icelandic, so that a computer becomes *tolva*—a "number prophetess" and television becomes *sjornvarp*—"view casting".

Icelandic is a highly inflected language, like Latin; its nouns and verbs change bewilderingly according to their grammatical position in the sentence. For example, the word *hestur*, "a horse", changes like this: *hér er hestur* ("here is a

Two Icelandic women producing traditional handwoven clothing and rugs are examples of the two types of Icelanders—those descended from the Vikings and those descended from the Celts

horse"); *um hest* ("about a horse"); *frá hesti* ("from a horse"); *til hesti* ("to a horse, on horseback").

The Icelandic alphabet contains thirty-three letters; most of these are pronounced as in English, but there are some Icelandic characters (for example, there is a form of *d* which is pronounced *th*), and there are some letters which have special Icelandic pronunciation (for example, *j* is pronounced like the English *y* in "yellow").

A modern school building. Iceland's standard of education is high and pupils learn foreign languages as a matter of course

Most Icelanders speak English, which is taught in all their schools, and they nearly all welcome a chance to practise it. Most also speak Danish and many speak some German; a few can speak French, Spanish and Russian. Iceland has splendid schools and one university (at Reykjavik). Some students also attend other universities in Western Europe to study special subjects. There are long summer holidays but during them many school-children work. Older students may also work in the fish industry and in many other jobs.

The Icelanders are great lovers of reading and they now have libraries for all the towns and the larger villages. Their ancient sagas form part of the world's great literature, and they have many modern writers (one of them, Halldor Kiljan Laxness, won a Nobel Prize in 1955), some of whose works have been translated into other languages. Iceland has excellent book-shops and, in proportion to the size of the population, a surprisingly large number of books are published in Iceland—more, per capita, than in any other country in the world.

Music also flourishes in Iceland; there are symphony orchestras, brass bands and choirs, and the younger people are as keen as those in other lands on the modern "pop" music and dances.

Iceland also has its artists and sculptors, its architects, its weavers, woodworkers and potters. It has excellent theatres and a number of cinemas. There is a State Broadcasting Service which, since 1966, has been operating a television service as well as the Icelandic radio service.

The Icelanders are very helpful to foreign visitors, but one custom may surprise newcomers—they never take "tips". A taxi-driver is paid by his fare, and does not expect anything else. There is no need to have a "whip round" for the driver after a coach tour: to suggest anything of the sort might give offence and be thought impolite. It would however be in order, if a taxi has taken you sight-seeing, or if the driver has been very helpful, to invite him to join you afterwards in a soft drink or a cup of tea and one of Iceland's delicious local cakes.

Another national custom might seem odd though it has been used in many lands. The term "Ben", found in so many Biblical names, simply means "son of", like the Scottish "Mac" and the Welsh "Ap". Similarly, an Icelandic man is called "the son of" and a girl "the daughter of" his or her father, using not the surname but the Christian name, and a girl keeps this name even after she marries.

Thus if John Blake, son of Thomas Jones, were to emigrate to Iceland, along with his son William and his daughter Edna, and become naturalised, he would be called not "Mr John Blake" but "Herra John Thomasson" (notice the two letter s); his son would become "Herra William Johnsson". All names in the telephone directory use not the surname but the Christian name, so that the two would appear respectively under J and W.

Similarly, "Miss Edna Blake" would become "Froken Edna Johnsdottir" until she married, when she would become "Fru Edna Johnsdottir", and she would appear in the directory under E. So if you wish to telephone anyone in Iceland, be sure that you know his or her Christian name.

If you have read Jules Verne's story *Journey to the Centre of the Earth*, you will remember how he wrote that about a hundred years ago the people of Iceland were very poorly dressed and seemed very unhappy. The men wore a coarse jersey made of the local black wool, a hat with a broad brim and trousers with a red stripe; their shoes were made of pieces of leather.

The girls wore a bodice and petticoat also of black wool and braided their hair and topped it with a little grey bonnet; the married ladies wrapped their heads in a coloured kerchief and wore a white linen scarf.

The men, though at times they gave a short spasmodic laugh, never seemed to smile. The womenfolk had pleasant faces but never seemed to show any expression. And all of them looked thoughtful, as though they felt themselves out of touch with the rest of humankind, poor exiles banished to an icy land which seemed fit only for Eskimoes.

All this *may* have been true, although Verne had never visited Iceland; if so, it shows what life was like when the country was under Danish rule. But now Iceland is free, and its people no longer look poor, lost or unhappy. They are content to be in their own land and are cheerful and enterprising. The faces of their womenfolk are still pleasant but they are *not* devoid of expression, for men and women alike are bright and energetic.

In a general way, the men are not very dressy, but this is not because of poverty; they do not fuss about their clothes any more than people of other nationalities do. But, when they wish, they can look as smart as the men of other lands. And the women of Iceland are as keen on "making the best of themselves" as women are elsewhere.

They have a national costume—a long black dress reaching almost to the ground, with a gold belt and edging.

Their costumes look very picturesque, but nowadays they are kept for special occasions like national festivals. If you ask an Icelandic girl if she looks like that when she goes dancing with her boy-friend she will laugh and shake her head.

A charming example of Iceland's national costume

The Icelanders are keen sportsmen, though some of their sports are practised only during the light summer months, for the winter days are too short to encourage much outdoor activity. The most popular sport is soccer, and many of the towns and villages have their own football pitches. Rugby is not played, and neither are baseball, cricket or lawn tennis. Indoor sports which are popular all the year round are basketball, handball, and shooting on the rifle range, as well as a little badminton and table tennis. Golf is becoming popular in Reykjavik and Akureyri, but except in summer it may be discouraged by the weather. There are a few rifle clubs, and there is one gliding club near Reykjavik. Athletics are popular, and most of the towns have their own sportsfields, with a running-track around the central football ground.

By law, all Icelandic children must learn to swim, though really there was no need to make this compulsory, for they enjoy the water as much as do their elders. There is little sea-bathing, for the coast is so rocky that there are only a few beaches, and the temperature of the sea water is rather on the low side. River bathing can provide some startling contrasts, for some of the streams are fed by melt-water from the glaciers and others by warm water from the hot springs. In the latter, though the rocks around may be covered with snow, the water is pleasantly warm. There are many natural swimming-pools and indoor swimming-baths, all with warm water. There are also some saunas (steam baths).

The favourite Icelandic winter sports include skating on the frozen lakes and ponds, and on the long sheltered fjords, like the one at Akureyri. In the north, there is a little skiing. Perhaps because sea-fishing is a serious business in Iceland there is not much pleasure-boating or yachting, but there are small boats and a few motor-boats on the larger lakes, as well as a little water-skiing and speed-boating.

Speed-boating on one of Iceland's many lakes. The summer "hut" flying the Icelandic flag is typical of such holiday homes. Note the "boathouse" to the left of the picture

Glima wrestling—the national sport of Iceland

Iceland has its own form of wrestling, the *Glima,* in which the wrestler wears a special belt and his aim is to throw his opponent by lifting him bodily or by tripping him; here strength and weight are less important than skill. Boxing is illegal in Iceland.

Hiking across the lava-field can be tiring, but across grassland it is as pleasant as elsewhere. This is a very popular pastime and there are a number of rambling clubs; the largest and most active is the Iceland Travel Association. Visitors are often welcome to join rambles. Rock-climbing and caving are undertaken only by enthusiasts.

Pony-trekking with Mount Snaefell in the background. Trekking is popular both with the Icelanders and with visitors

There are plenty of Youth Hostels in Iceland and many groups of Boy Scouts and Girl Scouts (*not* Girl Guides). The boys wear blue shorts, the girls a blue skirt. Pony-trekking is also popular and tours can be arranged.

The small sturdy Icelandic steeds are called not ponies but horses—for they are full size for Iceland! They are so small that a rider meaning to go any distance takes two horses, riding one and taking the other on a lead-rein; so that he travels in "relays". Provided the rider knows how to handle them, the horses are friendly and docile; they have five

34

"speeds": walk, trot, gallop (no canter), pace and running walk.

Tours on horseback can be arranged from Reykjavik and some other centres and may last a week or more, the riders putting up at the country hotels or at farms. It is also possible to go mountaineering in unknown regions, for not all of Iceland has been explored. This is, of course, a serious matter and needs special preparation and skilled leaders, for glaciers may have to be crossed and rock-climbing may be necessary on the cliff faces.

There are many rivers and lakes in Iceland, and they contain five types of fish: trout, salmon, char, eels and stickle-back.

A salmon leaping in the River Laxa, in south-west Iceland

No animal, not even a pet, may be imported into Iceland; neither may birds' eggs. The animals on the island have been so long separated from those of the rest of Europe that they might easily fall a victim to diseases to which foreign animals are immune. A dog or cat, or a farm animal, imported into Iceland might start a devastating plague among the local animals.

This does not mean that the Icelanders do not care for their pets. They do. Indeed, they are so fond of them that they do not want to take any risks. Although it is forbidden to keep dogs, except on farms, they are attached to their dogs and cats and to the docile Icelandic horses.

Living where the winter nights are so long, the Icelanders naturally love light and colour. The town streets are well-lit, and in the houses the rooms have large windows and are well decorated with pictures; and, the Icelanders being such great readers, they have plenty of books too.

As there is no coal or oil in Iceland, but only lignite (brown coal) and peat, the towns are lighted with power from "white coal"—electricity generated by water-turbines driven by the mountain torrents. Many districts get their hot water from the hot springs.

The beds are made up not with sheets and blankets but with duvets. In summer the evenings do not start getting dark in Reykjavik until about ten; further north they begin even later, so most people in Iceland sit up rather late—which means,

An eider duck, a familiar sight in some parts of Iceland (its down is used for the traditional duvets or quilts)

of course, that as a result few of them are early risers!

An Icelandic breakfast can be quite generous—perhaps three kinds of bread (white, brown, wholemeal or rye), toast and biscuits, tea and a glass of milk. The other meals may include fish, meat, potatoes and other vegetables. Tinned food has to be imported, so it is rather expensive. Special Icelandic dishes, which may surprise visitors, include shark, which has been buried in sand, and pickled whale blubber. More ordinary are smoked mutton, salted cod, pickled meats, dried fish eaten cold with butter, and singed and boiled sheep's head.

A favourite dish is *skyr* made from curdled milk; this is something like yoghourt. Much fresh milk is drunk; so is coffee, served with thin pancakes and cream or jam. The Icelanders also drink light beer, a schnapps called *brennivin* and, of course, soft drinks.

When drinking a friend's health, Icelanders raise their glasses and say *Skal!* at the same time they look into one another's eyes.

37

Reykjavik, Capital of Iceland

Even though Ingolfur Arnarson made his home at Reykjavik, it did not become an important town until about A.D. 1800 when small industries and the fisheries began to be developed. It had been granted a municipal charter in 1786, when it had only about two hundred inhabitants. By 1900 it had 11,600; it now has 85,000 out of a total population of 232,000.

It stands on a low peninsula pointing westward, to the south of Faxa Bay in south-west Iceland. Across the bay you can see Snaefell, which Jules Verne called "Sneffells" in his story *Journey to the Centre of the Earth*—but, alas, it is capped only with a glacier, and there is no crater leading down to the earth's centre!

Though its name means "Smoky Bay", Reykjavik is now almost smokeless, as it is heated mainly by hot water from underground. Only a small amount of the heating is oil-fired. The country near by is stony and barren, but the town is surrounded by mountains, and there are two islands a little way out in the bay.

At Reykir, about thirty kilometres (eighteen miles) east of the town, is the pumping station which supplies Reykjavik with its hot water. The water is purified and pumped across country in a massive pipe (wide enough to be walked on) encased in concrete. It is taken to big reservoirs at the summit of a low hill, from which it is then pumped down to the houses and offices, and to the warm swimming-baths.

A view of the residential part of Reykjavik, with the harbour and Mount Esja in the background

There are no woods in the town, but there are private gardens and parks. Most of the buildings are painted and have brightly-coloured roofs. In winter Reykjavik is surprisingly bright and clear. At night-time it is lit up not only electrically but also occasionally by the Northern Lights.

Verne mentioned, about a century ago, that almost all the buildings were small and squalid. That is no longer true. The houses are now modern—there are even a few skyscrapers —and there is the Parliament Building where the Al-Thing is now held. There are two cathedrals in Reykjavik, Lutheran Protestant and Roman Catholic. There are Cabinet Offices, the National Library, the University, the Museums, the

Harbour Building and Broadcasting House. There are statues of Jon Sigurdsson in the centre of a little park, of King Christian IX of Denmark, and of Hannes Hafstein, author and poet, who was the first Minister for Iceland to be resident in Reykjavik. Another, of Ingolfur Arnarson, stands on a grassy hill overlooking the central square and the harbour, while a statue of Leif Ericsson, who discovered America, stands on another hill in the heart of the city.

The Arbaer Folk Museum, on the edge of the city, contains a number of old houses, which help the visitor to understand what life used to be like in Iceland. It was built round an old farmhouse, and other ancient houses have been re-erected around this, and refurnished just as they used to be when they were actually in use. There is also an old-style smithy and carpenter's workshop. Here too are examples of the stone huts which formerly served as houses in a land where there was hardly any timber except what was washed up on the sea shore. Their walls consist of large roughly-shaped flints, held together not by mortar but by rammed earth; the

The National Museum in Reykjavik

Traditional houses with turf roofs (preserved as a museum)

roofs, to give greater warmth in winter, are covered with turf. As grass grows not only on the roof but on the earth in the walls, these huts look from a distance rather like natural mounds.

Some of these huts are built in groups of two or three, side by side. When a farmer found his hut too small for comfort, he simply built another alongside it and made an opening through the wall to serve as a door, and later he might add a third.

One of the most interesting buildings is a turf church which was brought from about 240 kilometres (150 miles) away. It dates from 1840 and there are only four others like it in the country. This is not simply a museum exhibit, however, for it is still used for religious services, and over a hundred couples have been married in it since it was brought to Arbaer. It is entered through a belfry-gate, and opposite it is the "bride's room" where the brides put on their wedding finery before the service.

41

The only locomotive engine in Iceland is here and, beside it, the country's only traction engine. Both were used early in the century for hauling blocks of stone when the harbour was being constructed, and now they are kept only as interesting museum specimens.

In the open spaces between the houses folk-dances are sometimes held and displays of Icelandic wrestling are given. The girls who act as guides wear their traditional costume, so they too help to show what life was like in the old days when these costumes were worn generally.

The engine is the only one in the museum because there are no railways in Iceland; nor are there any trams or any underground railways. There is, however, an excellent bus service in Reykjavik, with a number of local routes about the city and with long-distance coaches to various parts of the country. All are "single-deckers", and all are speedy and comfortable. Much internal travel is done on the small but very efficient planes of Icelandair. For air travel abroad they have much larger planes which are equally efficient.

There are several other museums in Reykjavik, including the National Museum, which has sections devoted to historical subjects, natural history, and the national art gallery. This gives a cross-section of Iceland's history and culture from the days of the country's first settlement. The Harbour Building houses pilots and others and its roof gives a good view of the harbour. The Einar Jonsson Gallery contains a collection of the works of that best-known of Icelandic artists; the

Asmundur Sveinsson Gallery similarly displays some of that sculptor's works.

There are several interesting places within easy reach of Reykjavik.

Bessastadir, about fourteen kilometres (about ten miles) to the south, was once the seat of the Danish Governor, and is now the official residence of the Icelandic President. The farm attached to it produces, among other things, eiderdown from the many eider ducks which nest there.

Here, too, is the church with interesting coloured windows representing scenes from Iceland's history, one of which shows St Brendan challenging the "demon blacksmith" with his uplifted crozier.

Bessastadir, the residence of the President. It was once the seat of the Danish Governor of Iceland

Krisuvik is also to the south of Reykjavik, about twenty-five kilometres (about fifteen miles) away. Here there are a number of hot springs and sulphur deposits, including a spring from which flows not water but molten sulphur, and a small pool of loathsome-looking black mud, which seethes and bubbles almost alarmingly. Here too there is a lake whose waters formerly rose and fell, and within which, at one time, no fish could live. But now, perhaps as the result of an earth-quake, it behaves normally.

Not far away a great steam-jet roars with tremendous power from a large pipe buried vertically in the earth. It is so powerful that, when the first attempt was made to "pipe" the steam, the apparatus was blown clean out of the ground! Later attempts were more successful, and the steam now roars not direct from the ground but from an iron cylinder like a small boiler. It seems a pity to have so much energy going to waste, and the engineers have a plan for leading the steam across country to heat the water of a small lake, which would then be used to supply hot water to a town near by; the only trouble is that this would involve expensive engineering.

Many important and beautiful places are conveniently reached from Reykjavik. Foremost among these is Thingvellir. This is the plain upon which the first Al-Thing was held, in a vast stretch of lava broken by deep rocky gorges and fringed by mountains, among them an extinct volcano. Glaciers are visible in the distance. Here, too, is the largest lake in Iceland.

A view of Thingvellir, now a National Park. Some of Iceland's most famous men are buried in the grounds of the little church

It contains many trout, and through it flows the River Sog, which is rich in salmon. Thingvellir—the Thing-plain—is, and well deserves to be, protected by the Government as a National Park.

45

Thingvellir—the lake on a fine winter's day

A short distance from Thingvellir, and further east, is Gullfoss, "The Golden Waterfall", said to be the most beautiful waterfall in the world.

It plunges over rocks in the glacial River Hvita in a series of cascades into a narrow canyon. In bright sunshine these cascades produce beautiful rainbows.

So magnificent is Gullfoss that a foreign company once wanted to buy it and to charge a fee for viewing it. But the

46

Icelandic Government prevented this by declaring it to be national property and available, without charge, to visitors.

Not far from Gullfoss is the Great Geysir. The earth here used to emit a great jet of steam and hot water quite regularly. It is no longer so regular, but in this area there are a number of smaller glaciers and hot springs. If you visit them you will have to be careful to follow the guide's instructions; some of these geysers are surrounded by a very thin layer of stone, produced where the hot water evaporated. If anyone trod on it, this layer might give way and the person might be badly scalded.

Gullfoss ("The Golden Waterfall") in south-west Iceland—probably the most beautiful waterfall in the world

The hot water from these springs is used in several ways. They heat greenhouses, houses, a hotel, a school and an outdoor swimming pool. Even the ground here is warm and is used as a "nursery"; trees planted in this soil thrive splendidly, and when they are sturdy enough they are transplanted elsewhere. The hot water is also led in pipes to irrigate the fields.

The greater part of Iceland's population, and of its resources, are concentrated in Reykjavik. Everywhere there are signs of the city's prosperity: import merchants dealing in all kinds of goods; motor showrooms; small factories. In the harbour there are row upon row of trawlers, and towering cranes. There are in fact, two harbours, one for the trawlers, the other for traffic

An outdoor swimming-pool. The water is warm since it comes from a natural hot spring

Icelandair planes being serviced at the airport in Reykjavik

from abroad. There is also a large airfield, surprisingly large
for so small a city. It was provided by the British Army when
they occupied Reykjavik during the Second World War,
and when they and the Americans left, the airfield remained—
for, after all, an airfield is hardly the sort of thing that a de-
parting army can pack up and take with it! It now caters for
domestic flights within Iceland, while Icelandair, which plies
between Iceland and Europe (including Britain), and
Icelandic Airlines, as well as smaller companies, which ply
between Iceland, Europe and America, use Keflavik Airport.
These and ships from overseas carry both passengers and goods
to and from the rest of the world.

But, above all, Reykjavik organises the control of the bound-
less energy, in hydro-electric power and in heat from the
earth. Important now, this is likely to become far more important in the future.

Akureyri and Other Icelandic Towns

Akureyri, the third largest town in Iceland, with a population of 13,600, is situated at the head of Eyjafjordur, the island's longest fjord, so that, while actually on the coast, it is fifty-five kilometres (thirty miles) from the open sea. The fjord opens to the north, and is flanked on both sides by high mountains, their tops covered with snow. Rivers and waterfalls rush down the valleys between the mountain summits. These look as if a giant had trimmed them off with a knife at about the same level; this is because they are not really separate peaks at all but the remains of a lofty plateau which has been grooved with channels by the weather, the glaciers and the streams.

There is a narrow strip of land on the west side of the fjord, with a level spit extending into the water, and it is here that most of the town has been built, including the airfield and, of course, the harbour. The town also extends to the lower slopes of the hills. This is the site of the Church, an imposing modern building—it stands at the top of a flight of one hundred and twelve steps, leading up from the top of a steep road. It has some fine stained glass windows; one is a survivor from Coventry Cathedral which was bombed in the Second World War; the others are from Exeter.

The town also contains the usual public offices, a library, several museums, two cinemas, and an open-air bathing-pool; this, like the indoor bathing-pool, gets its water from the hot springs. On a spur of the hill which dominates the town is a statue of Helgi the Lean and his wife, the first settlers in this region.

Akureyri forms an excellent centre from which to explore the north-west of Iceland. One especially attractive coach tour is to Lake Myvatn, 105 kilometres (65 miles) to the east. The coach laboriously climbs up a series of zig-zags, giving a splendid view of the town and the fjord. Having traversed a lofty plateau, the road then descends into the valley of the Eyjafjordur.

Here you will see one of the peculiarities of road travel in Iceland. Although the bridges across the streams and gorges are strong and well made, they were designed only to take motor-cars, for when they were built the use of coaches was unforeseen. They are so narrow that a coach which wants to cross them does so very carefully and slowly.

Lava formations at Lake Myvatn

An aerial view of Akureyri at the head of the Eyjafjordur, Iceland's longest fjord, which opens to the north

Crossing the bridge over the Eyjafordur brings the traveller to another of the country's finest sights. This is Godafoss— "the Fall of the Gods". It gets its name from the tradition that in A.D. 1000, when what we should now call the President of the Al-Thing was converted to Christianity, he showed that he had given up his faith in the old heathen gods by throwing his idols into the stream. Though only about twenty-five metres (thirty feet) high, the fall is very broad, with a tremendous flow of water that throws up a cloud of spray, tinted in the sunshine with rainbow colours.

In this valley the Government has made efforts to reafforest the land. There were formerly large areas of woodland here; but since the trees were too small to provide timber for building, many of them were used for fuel and the woods were almost destroyed. Although, in these days of hydro-electric power, wood is no longer needed as fuel, the Icelandic Government is anxious to grow new forests to replace those which have been destroyed.

Near Laugar (an educational centre with a boarding-school, warm springs, a swimming-pool and hot-houses), the road divides. To the north it leads to the sea at Husavik, and then along the coastal road to the east. About eight kilometres (five miles) from the junction is the Grenjadarstadur Folk Museum, installed in a large farmhouse built of turf.

Godafoss
("The Fall
of the Gods")

The other branch of the road leads in a north-easterly direction to Reykjoskoll, on the northern shore of Lake Myvatn. Here is the largest farm in Iceland—its area is twice the size of Luxemburg. Much of it, however, consists of lava on which little can grow. Even amidst the barren lava, though, there are small patches of soil and, as volcanic soil is very fertile, these are fenced off and used like allotments for growing potatoes.

The name Myvatn means "Midge Lake" and it is indeed the breeding-place of countless mosquitoes. Visitors must either wear gloves and a veil like a beekeeper, or cover their faces and hands with a fly-repellent preparation. Nuisance though the midges are, however, they attract myriads of ducks of different species, some not found anywhere else in Europe. Myvatn is indeed a bird-watcher's paradise, and ornithologists flock to it from far away.

The scenery around the lake is very striking. To the north is a prominent hill, and there are many smaller hills in the area called "pseudo craters", for although they look like the remains of former volcanoes they were really produced by the explosion of great bubbles of steam in the flowing lava. Some of them form islands, beautifully rounded, within the lake itself. Elsewhere, the lava has taken strange shapes, some like the remains of huge buildings, like those called "Black Castles", others resembling outlandish prehistoric beasts.

East of Myvatn the country is desolate, with hardly a village or a farm. At Namskarth, not far from the lake, there are hot springs, a horrible-looking pool of seething mud, and the pits of the old sulphur workings. Here another mineral is worked, with silt dredged up from the lake being used to make diatomite —one of the components of gunpowder. In the Middle Ages this region used to be mined for sulphur.

The lake is popular for rowing and speedboating, and journeys can be made from here to other interesting places by coach, or taxi or on horseback. There is good hiking, too, along the paths.

As a centre of commerce, Akureyri is anxious to vie with Reykjavik. It already has many advantages: it is the centre for a branch of the Icelandic co-operative movement, easily the largest employer in Iceland; it has factories for producing woollen textiles, for treating and exporting fish, for manufacturing other goods, for handling and distributing imports. And tourism is being developed, with glimpses of the Midnight sun, and splendid scenery within easy reach. Not far away,

Hot springs at Namskarth, to the east of Lake Myvatn

Fishing-boats in the harbour at Akureyri

too, there is unlimited potential energy in the form of subterranean heat. Akureyri is the obvious centre for developing local communication and trade; it has large harbours and a large airport.

Other significant towns in Iceland include:

HAFNAFJORDUR (Population: 12,000). Eleven kilometres (about five miles) from Reykjavik. It lies in the lava country, is sheltered from the cold north winds, and possesses a good harbour.

HUSAVIK (Population 2,500). A busy fishing port where one of the first Viking explorers landed. Several hot springs are near by, as is the geothermal power-station which supplies power to Akureyri. It has a coastal radio station for shipping and an interesting church. It also has good salmon fishing.

ISAFJORDUR (Population: 3,200). It is the main township of the western peninsula, with a harbour and a thriving fishing

56

industry, built on a spit in a short deep fjord. It is the best centre for visiting the area, with sea-trips off Cape Horn (North Cape), the most northerly point here.

KEFLAVIK (Population: 6,000). Near the Keflavik Airport, also the base of the U.S. forces in Iceland. It is one of Iceland's largest towns. It has a thriving port with a good harbour. In a somewhat bleak and barren area, this is interesting geologically because of the hot springs and its volcanic origin.

KOPAVOGUR (Population: 14,000). Almost a suburb of Reykjavik, it is the second largest town in Iceland. It has an interesting modern church of unusual design. Several light industries have been established here.

WESTMANN ISLANDS (VESTMANNAEYJAR) (Population: 5,000). There are daily sailings and an air service to Reykjavik. Supposedly named from the "West Men", Irish slaves of the early Vikings, who fled here from their masters. Only one island, Heimaey, is inhabited during the winter season. It is the most important fishing-centre in Iceland, because of the proximity of rich fishing-grounds for cod.

Isafjordur, built on a spit in a short fjord

The submarine volcanic eruption near the Westmann Islands in November 1963

The islands were the scene of Iceland's most recent volcanic eruptions, both of them remarkable. In November 1963 a vessel reported sighting a ship on fire to the west of Heimaey; there had been no other evidence for this, but a smell of sulphur had been noticed, and the sea in that area had been unusually warm.

Then it was realised that a new volcano had opened beneath the waves. As the water poured in upon the molten lava an immense column of smoke and steam had been formed, visible from Reykjavik. The new crater went on hurling out masses of ash and "volcanic bombs" and emitting lava.

These accumulated to form a new island, and soon some enterprising journalists landed upon it and unfurled a flag advertising the paper they worked for. To put an end to such proceedings, the Icelandic Government formally claimed the new island as part of their territory and gave it a name—as there was a giant in Norse mythology known as Surtur, the new island was called Surtsey—*ey* being Icelandic for "island".

Spores and other lowly forms of life were blown onto the island by the wind or brought over on the plumage or feet of birds, and slowly some of the lava broke down and formed soil; marine animals came to live among the off-shore reefs, and seals came out to bask upon Surtsey.

Anxious to study the development of the island's life, and to study the new volcano, teams of scientists landed upon

An aerial view of Surtsey, the island which suddenly appeared. The picture shows lava rivulets entering the sea

Surtsey, and some of them had an alarming experience. While they were on the island the volcano began to erupt, not only sprinkling them with glowing ash but pelting them with volcanic bombs, much as the Irish monks had been pelted centuries earlier. For some time the wind and sea prevented them from rowing away, so they had to stay on the island.

Another crater opened beside the first, and later two others opened beneath the waves; these also produced islets, but they were soon destroyed by the waves, whereas Surtsey itself seems

Boats leaving Heimaey on their way to the fishing-grounds—the harbour was actually improved by the eruption in 1973

to be permanent. It has grown greatly, and is well colonised by plant and animal life.

In 1973 yet another crater opened, this time on Heimaey itself. The town was largely destroyed by the lava emitted by the crater and by its showers of ash. It even seemed that the island's only harbour would be blocked. Many of the houses were swept away or buried, but fortunately there was no loss of human life.

The Icelanders fought the disaster with the same cool courage with which their ancestors had faced the great fissure eruption two centuries earlier. The inhabitants and much of their property were evacuated by sea and air to Iceland itself. Attempts were made to divert the flow of lava and to quench its heat by water-cannon; they were not completely successful, but they did reduce the destruction.

When the eruption was over, the people, again with the true Viking spirit, rebuilt their shattered homes and reoccupied them. The damage had been great, but it had not daunted them—and they found that the eruption had actually improved the entrance to their harbour!

Fishing, Farming and Other Industries

In the entrance hall of one of the largest hotels in Akureyri there is a plaque which shows two Icelandic families greeting one another, a farmer's family and a fisherman's family. This represents co-operation between Iceland's two great industries, farming and fishing. From Reykjavik and Akureyri, and from many another port and fishing-village along the coast, the sturdy trawlers put out to reap what has poetically been called "the harvest of the sea".

FISHING

Though the Icelandic trawlermen are equipped with all the modern navigational aids, including radar, their work involves as much risk as did that of their Viking ancestors, and they face this with the same courage and efficiency.

They not only fish off Iceland but go as far afield as the Newfoundland fishing-grounds and off the coasts of Greenland. Their chief catch is herring, cod and haddock, as well as capelin, shrimps and lobsters. Great scaffolds can be seen near the coasts of Iceland from which hang thousands of large fish, drying in the sun. The fish are cured in warehouses, salted or canned and exported to many parts of the world. They form the country's chief export.

The first Icelandic fishing craft were open rowing-boats. These were replaced by sailing vessels, and these in their turn were supplanted by motor-boats and trawlers.

Once herring was plentiful
during the season—
this picture was taken
at Siglufjordur

This has lengthened the herring season to about three
months during the late summer. The methods used have also
been improved. The shoals are located by means of sonar or
asdic, and the nets are hauled mechanically. This has had the
result of greatly increasing the catch, although in recent years
herring has become scarce because of over-fishing by other
nations.

In 1908 the first small freezing plant was installed in the
Westmann Islands; three years later the first factory started
work, converting the surplus herring catch into cattle meal.

Fishing is an extremely dangerous occupation in this region, for the coasts of Iceland are steep and rugged and they are swept by fierce storms in Arctic weather. In order to help any victims of a shipwreck, "survival huts" have been erected around the coasts, and these are available for anyone who needs help, Icelander or foreigner.

In about 1950 there began the first forebodings of what is now known as the "cod war". British trawlers were coming nearer and nearer to Iceland in order to fish, and the Icelandic skippers were beginning to think that their livelihood was threatened. The fishing industry is important to Britain, although she also has other industries. To the Icelanders, it is vital for, apart from farming, they have no other means of making a living.

The college which trains seamen in Reykjavik. The Icelanders, being an island people, are noted for their seamanship and expertise in fishing

In 1944, when Iceland had just gained independence from Denmark, the herring shoals started swimming further away from the coast. The Icelandic government therefore announced that in future Icelandic territorial waters would be extended, and the International Court of Justice supported this view.

The British protested, and for a time they imposed a ban on fish from Iceland, but at last they agreed to accept it. Then the fish started going even further away and, in 1958, Iceland extended her territorial waters still further from the shore. Britain, like several other nations, protested and declared that their trawlers would ignore this new limit and would send ships of the Royal Navy to make sure that the Icelandic fishery protection vessels did not interfere with British trawlers.

The Icelandic coastguard vessels now started to try to arrest the British trawlers, firing blank shots and even live shots aimed across their bows. The British trawlermen threatened to defend themselves with any weapon which came to hand, and the British Royal Navy frigates, which were faster and larger than the Icelandic gunboats, sailed between the gunboats and the trawlers. Each side accused the other of bad seamanship and reckless disregard for safety.

Slowly the mutual hostility died down, partly because traditionally the Icelanders had always been so ready to assist British crews in distress, since the Icelandic trawler crews were more used to these bleak northern waters.

In the 1970s, the dispute broke out again in a more violent

form. By this time the Icelanders had extended their territorial waters still further, and the British were more determined than ever not to recognise them. Again tempers became frayed, shots were fired, and there were minor collisions between Icelandic gunboats and Royal Navy frigates. Again there were mutual accusations of bad seamanship and disregard for human life. In October 1975 the territorial waters limit was further extended.

In 1976 the Icelandic government appealed again to NATO and threatened that if their appeal were disregarded they might not only break off diplomatic relations with Britain but even withdraw from NATO itself. A compromise situation was then reached.

WHALING

Some seventy-five kilometres (about forty-five miles) from Reykjavik, at the head of the Hvalfjördur Fjord, is the Whaling Station, where the whales caught at sea are hauled ashore. The whale meat is cut up and processed to produce animal food for export.

The whales are killed during the summer with a harpoon-gun fired into some vital part of their body. They are then pumped full of air to keep them afloat and, lashed alongside the whaler, they are taken to the Station. In a good season, several whale carcases may be floating off the Whaling Station—greyish masses in the bloodstained sea. Each in turn is hauled in by a mechanical winch up a sloping ramp.

Skinning a whale at the whaling-station in the Hvalfjördur fjord

When the whale reaches a level platform at the top of the ramp, work begins at once. The whale is skinned mechanically. The flesh and blubber are separated and are cut into lumps of suitable size with flensing-knives. Then the bones are cut into short lengths by mechanical saws.

The whole process is interesting but not pleasant to watch —and even less pleasant to smell! Yet it forms an essential part of Iceland's industry.

67

A rare sight in Iceland today where most of the cattle are of a breed which has no horns

FARMING

Although so much of Iceland's surface consists of sterile lava, there are areas of agricultural country, and these are efficiently cultivated. At one time, the farmers in the north used to drive their sheep over the mountains to Akureyri, but in 1881 they started to do business with a Scottish merchant, whose ships sometimes put in at Husavik, about forty kilometres (twenty-five miles) further east on the north coast. He insisted that the Icelanders should provide a landing-stage and a store.

In order to do this they formed a co-operative society. So the Scotsman bought their sheep, but instead of paying cash, he imported goods for the local people. The co-operative prospered wonderfully.

Now, many years later, it is the largest business in Iceland,

and about two-thirds of the people belong to it. It owns dairies, fishing-vessels and processing-plants, woollen goods factories, supermarkets and stores.

Farming is second only to fishing as the source of Iceland's prosperity. The farmhouses are no longer the crude stone and turf cottages of old. They have concrete walls and gaily-coloured corrugated roofs and are surrounded by their own farm-land.

Sheep are far more numerous than cattle; they are now sheared not by hand, as in the old days, but by machines. The hay is mown not by scythes but by modern harvesters. Even one of the farmer's oldest friends, the Icelandic horse,

Rounding up sheep

is being replaced by tractors and trailers. But nothing can replace the farmer's other friend, the Icelandic sheep-dog, a special breed.

During the bleak Icelandic winter, with its long nights, the sheep are housed under shelter. In the spring, having been marked in the ear with special identification marks to show to whom they belong, they are turned loose to graze in the mountains. Then, in the autumn, all the farmers in the district, with help from the townsfolk, get together to "round up" the sheep. This task demands skill and experienced leadership. It is hard work, although it makes a pleasant change for the university students and for others who for most of the time are cooped up in a factory, a school or an office.

Some of the sheep are reared for their fleeces, which are woven into warm woollen cloth; others for their lamb or mutton, either eaten in Iceland or canned for export. Others, the pick of the flock, are kept for breeding.

There are some poultry farms in Iceland, but these are valued chiefly for the eggs they produce. Chicken is not one of the Icelanders' favourite foods. Potatoes and other root crops are grown out in the open, but tomatoes and lettuce have to be cultivated in greenhouses warmed by the hot springs. Most of the food produced on the farms is for home consumption, but some of the meat, butter and cheese is for export. On the other hand, most of the fruit and tinned food eaten in Iceland has to be imported. The milk from the dairy cattle is, of course, for home consumption. Icelanders, adults as well as children,

Grapes growing in a hothouse warmed by water from the hot springs

drink large quantities of it. Some, when curdled, forms *skyr*, a kind of yoghourt, which is also very popular. Lamb and mutton form part of the Icelanders' usual diet.

71

Though the lava itself is sterile, the soil it produces when it is broken down by the weather and mixed by the wind and rain with ordinary soil is very fertile indeed.

OTHER INDUSTRIES

Though fishing and farming form the largest of Iceland's industries, others are now growing in importance. Some are a by-product of farming: the manufacture of wool and woollen products, including blankets, scarves, caps and gloves; and of carpets, mainly of wool. From farm animals come not only meat but leather and sheepskins; also butter, cheese and *skyr*. From fishing come fish, salted, dried, frozen or canned.

Most of the industries, however, derive from the country's mineral wealth. Easily the most important is cement. Then comes aluminium. The most important *natural* product is diatomite, small fossil shells from the bottom of Lake Myvatn, which are heated to form kieselguhr, a component of gun-powder, by use of geothermal steam (produced by the earth's internal heat). Pumice-stone is also quarried for export in smaller quantities.

Fertilisers form an important industry. Paints and varnishes are also produced, as are nails, glass, pottery and chocolate.

Studies are being made of the prospects for other industries. One is the "sea chemicals project", to produce salt and chlorides from geothermal brine on the Reykjanes peninsula to the extreme south-west of Iceland. By using geothermal steam, it should be possible to produce soda ash from the magnesium chloride in the brine, and this could be transformed into the metal magnesium and chlorine, both very important to industry.

Shipbuilding is, of course, a very important industry in Iceland, and is carried on in many places around the coast. At first, the shipyards were mainly kept busy with repairs but, since 1965, fishing-boats have also been built, and some of these are sold abroad.

All towns and villages in Iceland have electricity supply and more than half of Iceland's farms are electrified, some of them having their own generators. This is largely possible because there is so much water power and so much geothermal energy. It is hoped to harness much more of both, but some energy still has to be imported in the form of oil.

By drilling deep bore-holes, and in other ways, the geothermal regions are being explored. Schemes are being prepared for using this energy to heat more towns and also to heat greenhouses with natural hot water. The natural energy is also used to produce metals from ores imported from abroad, to be re-exported to the places from which they came.

Iceland's Flag, National Anthem and National Holidays

When Iceland was still under Danish rule, it flew the Danish flag—a white cross on a red field, just the reverse of England's Cross of St George.

Not until 1913 did the King of Denmark allow Iceland to have its own flag, and not until 1918 did he allow it also to be flown at sea. The flag of Norway places a blue cross down the centre of a white cross similar to that of Denmark. The Icelandic flag is the exact reverse of this—a red cross edged with white on a blue field. The Icelanders say that these are the natural colours of their country: red for the volcanic fires, white for the icefields, and blue for the sea.

The President of Iceland has his own standard. At the centre of the Government Flag, which is like the National Flag except that it ends in swallow-tails, it places a shield bearing the country's arms: a dragon, a vulture, a giant and a bull—creatures which have long been regarded as Iceland's guardian spirits. There is a legend that an evil spirit in the form of a whale sent to attack Iceland found the country protected by these fearsome monsters.

Iceland's national anthem was composed in 1874 by the poet Matthias Jochunsson, to celebrate the thousandth anniversary of the settlement of Iceland; the music was composed by Sveinbjorn Sveinbjornsson. It is known as *O, God vors land* (Oh, Iceland's God, Our Country's God).

Iceland has many public holidays. On Twelfth Night, the

last day of Christmas, decorations are taken down and there are parties and celebrations. Early in the year begins the old month known as *Thorri*. It is associated with pickled and smoked Icelandic food specialities. Parties are popular at this time, and at these schnapps is usually drunk.

The Monday before Shrove Tuesday is called *Bolludagur*. Children "beat" adults with coloured sticks to get *Bollur* (cream buns); everyone eats lots of them. On Shrove Tuesday, which is known as *Sprengidagur* ("Bursting Day") salted mutton and thick pea soup are popular. On Ash Wednesday children tie little bags of ash on the backs of unwary adults. This is especially popular in Akureyri, where the children also wear masks and collect money for charity.

Iceland's flag features in the celebration of National Day, in Reykjavik

The third Thursday in April is regarded as *Sumardagurinn fyrsti*, the First Day of Summer. It is greeted with carnival queen processions and general rejoicing in Reykjavik—and no wonder, as night lasts almost all day in winter!

The first of May is Labour Day, as in many other countries. It is marked by Trade Union and other workers' processions, political speeches, and brass bands, especially in Reykjavik.

June 17th is Iceland's National Day, to mark Iceland's final break with Denmark and gaining of complete independence in 1944. There are processions, and the Boy and Girl Scouts parade with their flags. In Reykjavik they line the walks in the Central Park which surrounds the statue of Jon Sigurdsson, facing the Parliament building. After attending service in the Cathedral the President makes a speech from the balcony of the Parliament building, and then he lays a wreath at the foot of the statue.

When the ceremonies are over the day is devoted to recreation. In Reykjavik, a platform is erected on the hill dominating the city centre and here, during the afternoon, an entertainment is organised for the young people. On the sports field there are races, and competitions in jumping, *glima* wrestling, and other athletic events. During the evening, there is dancing in the city streets, and this continues almost all night until the small hours of the morning.

During the first weekend in August comes *Thjodhatid Vestmannaeyja* (Westmann Islands National Day). When Iceland was granted Home Rule by the king of Denmark in 1874

Scouts
at the
statue of
Jon Sigurdsson
in Reykjavik on
National Day

bad weather kept the islanders from taking part in the national celebrations so they decided to hold their own locally. This became traditional. They erect tents for themselves and their visitors and two days' sports are held with amusements, dancing, eating and drinking in the open air.

Seaman's Day, early in June, is however a national event. It is dedicated to Iceland's seamen and includes speeches, rowing competitions and displays of life-saving.

Leif Ericsson Day (though not a national holiday), on October 9th, celebrates the discovery of North America by that adventurous Viking. This celebration used to take place in Reykjavik, and Americans and Icelanders held a ceremony at his statue on its hill.

Late in October comes *Fyrsti vetrardagur* (Beginning of Winter) but, quite understandably, the Icelanders do not regard this as an occasion for ceremony!

On December 1st is the national celebration of the day when, in 1918, Iceland gained its independence from Denmark while still acknowledging the sovereignty of the Danish king. It is especially celebrated by the students.

As in other lands December 24th, Christmas Eve, is celebrated. But in Iceland the celebrations are quiet home affairs; entertainments outside are very unusual. It is on this day, and not on Christmas Day itself, that presents are given. The favourite dishes are *hangikjot* (smoked mutton), ptarmigan, and rice pudding. Christmas Day is more a religious festival.

New Year's Eve, December 31st, is the occasion for huge bonfires to be lighted at midnight throughout the country, and for fireworks to be let off; there is a brilliant display of them in Reykjavik.

Flags are flown on New Year's Day, Easter Sunday, the first day of summer, Labour Day, Whit Sunday, the National Day, June 17th, and Independence Day, December 1st, the President's birthday and Christmas Day. On Good Friday flags are flown at half mast.

Midnight celebrations for National Day in the Westmann Islands

Some Notable Icelanders

Few Icelanders have achieved world fame, but some at least deserve to have done so. Foremost among these is surely Leif Ericsson (Leifur Eiriksson), also known as "Leif the Lucky". He was the son of Eric the Red, who is reputed to have been rather a turbulent character. Forced to leave Norway, he went to Iceland; and forced to leave Iceland, he then went to Greenland. Such reputations are not always deserved, however; as Jules Verne put it, perhaps Eric the Red was no more red than Greenland is green.

Hearing that another Viking had seen some unknown land further west, very rich in timber, Eric decided to explore it. But, as he was going down to his ship, his horse threw him and he sprained his ankle. Taking this as an omen that he was not meant to discover any more lands, he sent his son Leif to lead the expedition instead. Leif first sighted a bleak barren land of flat rocks leading up to the ice mountains. Deciding that this was no use to them, he turned southwards, leaving behind the place he called "Stoneland". After three days, the expedition saw that the nature of the land had changed; there was much timber, so Leif called it "Woodland". A few more days brought them to another land, "where the dew tasted sweet"; as there were many grapes growing there, Leif decided that this should be "Vineland the Good". (These may have been Labrador, Nova Scotia, and part of New England.)

A reconstruction of
a Viking house
built at the time
of Leif Ericsson

Taking on board a cargo of grapes and timber, Leif returned to Greenland. Vineland was soon being colonised, but there was increasing trouble with the Skraelings, who may have been Eskimoes or Red Indians, or both.

So the colonies had to be abandoned, and their very sites are now unknown. But their traditions lived on and may have spurred other explorers to sail westward in search of this unknown land.

Christopher Columbus is rightly honoured as a great explorer. But if he was great, surely Leif Ericsson was far greater, for Columbus had the traditions of early discovery to urge him on, whereas Leif was sailing into the unknown. Indeed, not only Leif but the "great Vikings" who first explored Iceland must be regarded as great, as well as the Irish monks who first visited it: Naddodd, Garda, Floki, Ingolfur Arnarson who founded Reykjavik, and Helgi the Lean who founded Akureyri.

Our knowledge of these explorations comes from one of the Icelandic sagas, the *Landnamabok* (the Book of Settlement).

A view of Rafnseyri, the birthplace of Jon Sigurdsson

Jon Sigurdsson, who won Iceland's freedom from Denmark, also deserves to be considered a great man. So does Snorri Sturlusson, Iceland's greatest poet, and once President of the Al-Thing. He wrote poetry, prose historical works, and a life of St Olaf, early in the thirteenth century. Arni Magnusson was another eminent Icelandic scholar. There have also been several modern writers of repute—poets, dramatists and novelists—including Laxness, who won the Nobel Prize for Literature.

The term "Saga" is nowadays used rather loosely but it is really an Icelandic word meaning a prose narrative which is both story and history. It was developed in Iceland during the early Middle Ages. The sagas are the life-stories of individuals, families or larger groups of people. They are marked by their vivid and dramatic style; they may include humour or tragedy, but little romance.

Many were composed by Snorri Sturlusson and, old as they are, they can still be read by modern Icelanders, for the language has changed very little since they were written. Story-telling used to be very popular in Iceland both among the rulers and the ordinary folk, and if the sagas were not so splendidly written they might be called folk stories. They were recited before they were written down and they describe events which had happened years before.

Our knowledge of the early religion of Iceland, before it was converted to Christianity comes from the sagas. The King of the gods was Odin All-Father, who had sacrificed one of his eyes for the gift of knowledge and the power of foretelling the future. Thor was the god of thunder, and his weapon, the Hammer, represented the thunderbolt; when he buckled his belt tighter his strength was redoubled. Tyr was the god of war. The chief of the goddesses was Odin's wife, Frigg. Baldur the Beautiful was the sun-god, the son of Odin and Frigg. All these were among the Aesir, the gods who cared for mankind. There was no devil, but Loki, the god of fire, was also the god of malicious practical jokes. His wife was Angrboda.

There was no need to imagine a devil for the Icelanders; they had quite enough natural enemies! The earliest Vikings to arrive were of course used to snow and ice, but earthquakes and volcanoes were new and very terrible to them.

Religion in Iceland

The sagas were not thought of as mere stories: they expressed the Vikings' actual religious beliefs. Thor, Odin and the others were literally regarded as gods. But Odin All-Father was not thought of as the Creator: he was the Father only of men, not of the animals and certainly not of the giants and trolls; nor had he made the world. Moreover, he was not supposed to be almighty. He has been called the "god of anxiety", for he foresaw that some time in the future mankind and practically the whole of nature would be almost completely destroyed.

The Vikings believed in a life after death, but only for heroes; they were carried by the Valkyrie, Odin's warrior-maidens, to Valhalla, where the slain warriors feasted in Asgard, the home of the gods. It was situated at the summit of Bifrost, the rainbow. But even this would be destroyed, with almost everything else, at Ragnarok, the Day of Doom, when heaven and earth would come to an end. It was the task of the gods, and especially of Odin, to postpone this doom for as long as they could. But everyone knew it could not be postponed for ever, and when it did come the only thing for a Viking hero to do would be to decide to die with Odin.

Then the land would be swallowed up by the sea, but first it would have been consumed by the flames from Muspelheim, the Land of Fire, and so would come the end. One man, Lifthresir, and one woman, Lif, would escape the fire and the flood, and from them, when even the gods had perished, a new race of fair people would be born and all would be happiness.

It is easy to imagine that, compared with this gloomy prospect, the Gospel of Christ would seem wonderful, almost too good to be true; but it *was* true, the Christian missionaries assured them, and at last many of the Icelanders were converted. These missionaries had mostly been sent to convert them in the tenth century by the Norwegian kings, especially King Olaf Trygvason. The Icelanders adopted Christianity at the Thingvellir Al-Thing in A.D. 1000, but those who wished to keep to the old religion were allowed to do so—as long as they worshipped only in private.

Among the converts was the President of the Al-Thing, who proclaimed his new faith dramatically by casting the images of his former gods into Godafoss waterfall.

Within a century, Iceland had its own bishopric, at Skalholt for South Iceland and soon afterwards another was founded, at Holar, for North Iceland.

Godafoss—the falls are not very high but they are very beautiful

The Reformation was imposed upon Iceland by her Danish rulers, and the last of the Catholic Bishops was be-headed—without a trial—in the sixteenth century. The wealth of the monasteries was taken over by the Danish king. This impoverished the country while adding to the power of the king and placing the Icelanders more completely under his thumb.

Towards the end of the eighteenth century the whole country was united in one diocese, that of Reykjavik. Iceland is still a Protestant country with an established Church, the Evangelical Lutheran Church. There is however complete religious freedom, and members of the other denominations and religions are as highly regarded as the Evangelical Lutherans. These have a Cathedral at Reykjavik; it was erected in about the middle of the nineteenth century, but its predecessor was far older.

Reykjavik also has a Roman Catholic Cathedral, with its own school and modern hospital; and there are several convents in Iceland.

Most of the other Lutheran churches, some of which are quite ancient, have the usual corrugated iron roof and walls, and a small spire. The spire and the roof are usually green or red, the corrugated iron walls are white. The altar and the pulpit are brightly decorated.

There is an interesting church at Thingeyrar, where the first monastery in Iceland was founded in 1133. In contrast with this building is the very modern church at Husavik. The church

A typical turf-built church in northern Iceland

at Holar has a very high tower. Not far away is Grof, or Grafarkirkja, a church built of turf and dating from late in the seventeenth century. Another unusual church is at Kopavogur, not far from Reykjavik. The light from a small church, Strandarkirkja, near Thorlakshofn, is reputed to have saved seamen from shipwreck. There is another tiny turf church, about one hundred and forty years old, at Vidimyri.

Iceland in the Modern World

In some respects Iceland is almost unique, and its effects on the modern world are likely to be unusual—and extremely important. Several other countries have regions where the earth's crust is so thin that they are likely to have volcanic eruptions and earthquakes. In Iceland, almost the whole of the earth's crust is thin. It is almost cleft by a great crack in the earth's crust, and at any time that crack may split the island into two. This may not happen in the near future but it might happen at any time. The effects would be an immense fissure eruption with a great outpouring of lava, far-reaching earthquakes, the emission of poisonous fumes and showers of volcanic ash and bombs.

Nonetheless, this thinness of the earth's crust has certain advantages. Lacking in coal or natural gas, Iceland is well provided with energy, both from its geothermal steam and from its hydro-electric generators. For this reason it has no need to import much fuel, as most other nations have to do, and this gives it a strong position economically.

Its smaller industries are being developed, so that it may not, in the future, have to depend almost entirely on fishing and farming. The Icelanders are both intelligent and enterprising, and they should be able to profit from the experience gained in other lands and to develop their industries in quite unexpected ways.

Already ores have been sent to Iceland by other nations so

The eruption of Mount Hekla in 1970. Iceland is prone to such eruptions because of the thin earth crust in this region

that they can be smelted quickly and cheaply by geothermal energy and this could be done to a much greater extent, thereby greatly increasing Iceland's wealth.

The morning glow on Iceland's highest peak—just one example of her magnificent scenery

Iceland's scenery is so fine that when this is more widely known it should attract many more visitors. It ranges from mountains, volcanoes, elevated plateaux and glaciers to great and spectacular caves.

Apart from its scenery the other attractions of Iceland are its facilities for motoring and hiking, for fishing and boating, for bathing in naturally-heated pools and streams, and above all for pony-trekking on the friendly Icelandic horses. More energetic tourists might even like to give a hand on the farms at harvest time, or when the sheep are rounded up, or even to work, along with the students, at the whaling station or on a trawler.

Crossing a river on the small but sturdy Icelandic horses

A view of Reykjavik—halfway between New York and Moscow

During the Second World War the Americans are said to have thought of Britain as "an unsinkable aircraft-carrier off the coast of France". On the same lines we could think of Iceland as "an unsinkable aircraft-carrier in the North Atlantic". And the Icelanders, who at the end of the First World War had declared that never would they take part in any war, found, in the middle of the Second World War, that they were in too important a position to stay out. They were occupied first by the British and then by the Americans to keep them from being occupied by the Germans.

Iceland is still in that same position, with its capital almost half-way between New York and Moscow. So we can well be thankful that the Icelanders are so intelligent and enterprising, that they have a good system of education, and take world affairs and their own responsibility so very seriously.

Index